Fresh & Fun

May

BY JACQUELINE CLARKE

SCHOLASTIC
PROFESSIONAL BOOKS

NEW YORK • TORONTO • LONDON • AUCKLAND • SYDNEY
MEXICO CITY • NEW DELHI • HONG KONG

For my parents—

who have given me a personal history

to be proud of!

"It's Spring!" by Leland B. Jacobs. From JUST AROUND THE CORNER: POEMS ABOUT THE SEASONS, revised edition by Leland B. Jacobs. Copyright © 1993 by Allan D. Jacobs. Reprinted by permission of Henry Holt and Company, LLC.

"Safety in Numbers" by Jacqueline Clarke. Copyright © 2000 by Jacqueline Clarke. Used by permission of the author.

Produced by Joan Novelli
Front cover, interior, and poster design by Kathy Massaro
Cover and interior art by Shelley Dieterichs
Poster art by Jane Conteh-Morgan

ISBN 0-439-21609-5
Copyright © 2000 by Jacqueline Clarke
Printed in the U.S.A.
All rights reserved.

Contents

May delivers several invitations for celebrating and learning! Take advantage of these seasonal changes and events with the activities in this book, organized by four topics that are just right for this time of the year: Safety, Seeds and Flowers, Be Kind to Animals, and All About Me.

As you begin to spend more time outdoors, recognize the need for SAFETY by introducing children to bicycle, water, playground, and traffic safety rules. (See pages 6–11.) Coordinate activities in SEEDS AND FLOWERS (see pages 12–20) with the blooms of your school garden or neighborhood to let children discover their state flower, their birthday flower, the world's biggest flower, and the meanings of several flower names. Honor BE KIND TO ANIMALS WEEK with activities that introduce fictional and real animals. (See pages 21–26.) Use the ALL ABOUT ME section to reintroduce children to themselves and celebrate Personal History Month. (See pages 27–32.)

Here's what you'll find in the pages that follow:

- ❀ a reproducible send-home activity calendar
- ✿ literature connections
- ❀ pocket chart poetry
- ✿ a reproducible mini-book
- ❀ a math story mat
- ✿ a no-cook recipe
- ❀ hands-on science activities
- ✿ a pull-out poetry poster with a four-week lesson plan
- ❀ collaborative books
- ✿ collaborative banner
- ❀ computer connections, including an Internet scavenger hunt
- ✿ easy-to-learn poems and songs
- ❀ movement activities
- ✿ a rhyming mini-play
- ❀ and more amazing activities for May!

TIP

Throughout this book, you'll find web site suggestions to support various activities. Please remember that Internet locations and contents can change over time. We cannot guarantee the availability of sites recommended in this book at the time of publication.

Multiple Intelligences Connections

Your students learn in different ways—some are more verbal, others prefer written expression. Some are comfortable working in groups, others like independent projects. Some children's strengths lie in music, art, and other modes of expression. To help you meet your students' needs and encourage all of their strengths, you'll find all these learning modalities woven into the activities in this book.

Name _____

May Activity Calendar

Choose _____ activities to do each week this month.
Ask an adult in your family to initial the square in the box of each activity
you complete. Bring this paper back to school on _____ .

Monday	Tuesday	Wednesday	Thursday	Friday
Write the word May on a sheet of paper. List as many words as you can that end in -ay.	Look at this flower. Find a matching flower on this page.	Write down the foods you ate today. Count the fruits. Count the vegetables.	May is the fifth month. Name the fourth month. Name the sixth month.	A robin can beat its wings two times every second. How many times can it beat its wings in a minute?
Pretend you're a bird. How many times can you flap your wings in a minute?	Look for weather information in a newspaper. Find a weather prediction for tomorrow.	Tell someone at home a story about your day. Include a beginning, a middle, and an end.	Circle each Thursday on the calendar this month. The numbers make a pattern. Add three numbers to continue the pattern.	Look around you. Find something that comes in twos. Find something that comes in fives. What comes in tens?
List the foods you ate today. Draw a picture that shows how you feel about the foods you ate.	Make a map of the place you live. Draw what is in front, behind, to the left, and to the right of your home.	What do you think this means: April showers bring May flowers. Do you think this is true? Why or why not?	Look at the words on this page. Find one that sounds the same as the word two but has a different spelling.	Plan a pet show. (You can use a stuffed animal if you like.) Tell how you care for your pet. Tell what is special about your pet.
Look at the words on this calendar. Can you find one that rhymes with May?	Look out a window. Describe or draw ten things that you see. Use lots of detail.	Use your senses! List the sights, sounds, tastes, smells, and textures (the way things feel) that remind you of home.	Put an object in a sock. Let a family member try to guess what it is by feeling the object through the sock. Trade places. Play again.	Turn May into a tongue twister! Make up a sentence using as many words as you can that start with m.

Fresh & Fun May Scholastic Professional Books

5

Safety on the Playground

by Lucia Raatma (Bridgestone Books, 1999)

Use this book to review playground safety—including ways to avoid accidents (such as wearing clothes with no strings), going down the slide feet first, and using both hands while climbing.

This activity may also be used to reinforce water, bicycle, and traffic safety rules.

LANGUAGE ARTS

Rebuilding the Rules

Reinforce playground safety rules with this sentence-building activity.

◎ Write each playground rule on a sentence strip. Place the rules in the pocket chart and share them with children.

◎ Cut apart each rule word by word. Place one of the mixed-up rules in the pocket chart. Read it aloud to children. Ask: *What's wrong with this rule?* Let them help you rebuild the rule by putting the words back in the correct order. Encourage them to use clues such as capital letters and punctuation to identify the first and last word in the sentence.

◎ Write each rule on the outside of an envelope and place the cut-up words inside. Let children practice rebuilding the rules independently.

I Read Symbols and I Read Signs

by Tana Hoban (Greenwillow, 1983)

Both books use colorful photographs to help children discover the world of signs and symbols. As you explore each book, invite children to read the signs and symbols with you. When they go home that evening, encourage them to notice the signs and symbols in their neighborhood. Ask them to draw a picture of one and bring it back to school to share.

MATH, LANGUAGE ARTS, ART

Safety in Numbers

Share the poem "Safety in Numbers" (see page 11) to teach children that when playing outdoors they should use the buddy system and travel in groups. Guide children in following these directions to make an accordion-fold chain of paper people to use with the poem.

◎ Using an 8- by 11-inch sheet of construction paper, make four 2-inch accordion folds from left to right.

◎ Draw the outline of a person on the folded paper, making sure that the arms extend to the sides of the paper. Cut out the person, leaving the sides intact (so the chain will stay joined together when the paper is unfolded).

◎ Open up the paper chains. Color the first paper person (front and back) to look like you. Color the rest (front only) to look like your friends.

◎ Have children fold up the paper chains. As you read the poem aloud, have them open up the chain to reveal first themselves, then a buddy, and then a group. Let children bring their paper chains home with a copy of the poem to share with families.

ART

Dressed for Safety

Outdoor activities such as bike riding and roller-blading require children to wear protective equipment and clothing that allow them to be easily seen. Help children learn to dress for safety by designing clothes and equipment for a one-dimensional figure.

◎ Give each child a sheet of brown craft paper that covers the length and width of their body. Ask them to lie down on the paper while a teacher, parent volunteer, or classmate traces around them.

◎ Have them cut out the figure and add features such as eyes, nose, mouth, ears, and hair.

◎ Provide materials such as reflector tape and brightly colored (or fluorescent) paper, paint, and markers for children to dress the figure. Have children equip their figure with a helmet, knee pads, elbow pads, and other safety equipment and clothing. Display "safety kids" in the hallway to remind others how to dress while playing outdoors.

Franklin's Bicycle Helmet
by Paulette Bourgeois (Scholastic, 2000)

Beaver makes fun of Franklin's new bicycle helmet. Now he's ashamed to wear it. Rabbit comes to the rescue with words of encouragement and helps Franklin put things into perspective.

Teacher Share

SCIENCE

Why a Helmet?

Our skull protects our brain in the same way that a shell protects an egg. Sometimes, however, this protection is not enough. Demonstrate the need for a helmet with this experiment.

- Take children outdoors. Drop a hard-boiled egg from a height of ten inches. Ask children to describe what happened to the egg. Explain that our skulls can crack, just like the egg, and that is why we wear helmets for additional protection.

- Back in the classroom, form small groups and give each group an egg. Challenge them to use recycled materials (e.g., egg cartons, polystyrene, tape, paper, cotton, and so on) to create a safety device that will protect the egg when dropped on a hard surface.

- Take children outdoors and let them test their devices. Discuss the results. Compare and contrast the materials used with those found in a bike helmet. Invite children to share some of the activities for which they wear helmets (such as bike riding, skating, skateboarding, horseback riding, skiing).

Bob Krech
Dutch Neck School
Princeton Junction, New Jersey

SCIENCE

Staying Afloat

Children know that some objects sink while others float. Help them discover why this is true and how floating objects contribute to water safety.

◎ Gather children around a tub of water. Show them an empty, capped 20-ounce soda bottle. Ask them to predict whether it will sink or float. Place the bottle in the water and push it below the surface. Ask children to describe what happens.

◎ Fill the bottle halfway with water, cap it, and place it back into the tub. Again, let children predict whether it will sink or float, then describe what happens when you push the bottle under water.

◎ Finally, fill the bottle completely with water and cap it. Let children make their predictions. Place the bottle in the tub and observe the results.

◎ Ask children why the bottle sometimes floated and sometimes sank. Explain that for something to float, it must contain enough air to make it less dense than the water. As the air in the soda bottle was replaced with water, it became more dense, and, therefore, began to sink.

◎ Objects that float—such as kickboards, inner tubes, and life jackets— are important for water safety because they can help save someone from drowning. Our bodies are also able to float. Let children share their experiences learning to do a back float.

Book Break

Safety on Your Bicycle
by Lucia Raatma (Bridgestone Books, 1999)

Using photographs and simple text, this book teaches children how to stay safe while riding a bicycle. Includes information on safety checks, traffic rules, and the proper use of equipment.

Stopping/
Slowing Down

Right
Turn

Left
Turn

Simon Says, "Stop!"

Help children practice the hand signals for bike riding by playing Simon Says. Begin by teaching them the signals for left turn, right turn, and stopping/slowing down. (See right.) Once children know the signals well, play Simon Says by naming a signal for them to make. Children should follow only those commands preceded by the words "Simon Says."

TIP

Check for allergies
before serving.

SOCIAL STUDIES, SNACK

Stop-and-Go Snacks

Red, yellow, green! What do they mean? As children prepare this snack, they'll learn the significance of the colors in a traffic light. Each child will need a graham cracker, one tablespoon peanut butter, and three M & M's® (red, yellow, and green). Have children spread peanut butter on the graham cracker and place the M & M's® in a vertical position, with red on top, yellow in the center, and green at the bottom. Discuss what each color means, then "give the green light" to go ahead and eat the snack!

MUSIC AND MOVEMENT

Left or Right?

Many of the safety rules children must follow require them to know the difference between right and left. Share this poem and let children follow the actions as indicated in the rhyme to reinforce these directions.

Right Hand, Left Hand

This is my right hand,
I'll raise it up high.
This is my left hand,
I'll touch the sky.
Right hand, left hand,
Roll them around.
Left hand, right hand,
Pound, pound, pound.

Author Unknown

Name ______________________ **Activity Page** Date ______________________

Safety in Numbers

Sometimes it's great,
to play all alone,
building houses of blocks,
in a room of my own.

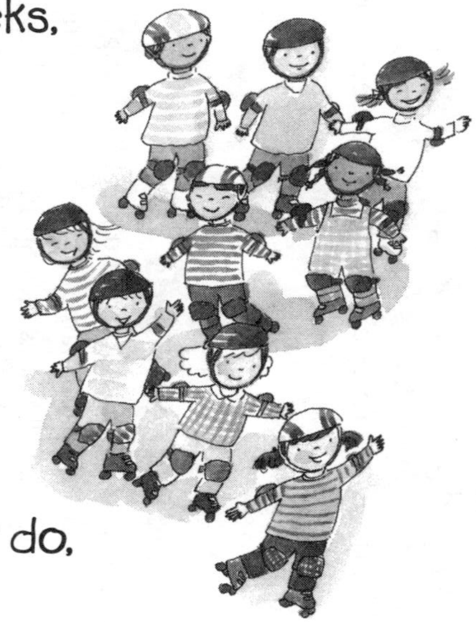

But when I go out,
to swim, skate, or ride,
I bring along a buddy,
to be by my side.

Then there are times,
When one buddy won't do,
I travel in groups,
to the park, mall, or zoo.

There's safety in numbers,
you can't go wrong.
When you leave the house,
bring your friends along!

—Jacqueline Clarke

Try This!

Draw a picture of you and a buddy. Write a sentence about what you are doing together.

____

____

Teaching With the Poster: "It's Spring!"

Snapdragon, snap,
Toadstool, turn,
Pussy willow, purr,
Fireweed, burn,
Black-eyed Susan, wink,
Sweet William, sing,
Forget-me-not, remember
It's Spring! Spring! Spring!

Catnip, nip,
Dandelion, roar,
Dogwood, bark,
Pitcher plant, pour,
Bee balm, buzz,
Bluebell, ring,
Jack-in-the-pulpit
Preach today,
It's Spring! Spring! Spring!

—*Leland B. Jacobs*

Children will learn what fun plant names can be as you share this spring poem with them.

Week 1: Find It in a Field Guide

Display the poetry poster and read aloud the poem with children. Display the poster along with assorted field guides, large index cards, crayons, and markers. Invite children to find information about each flower, including a picture. Have children draw pictures of the flowers on index cards and record facts, then display them around the poster.

Week 2: Act It Out

Once again, read the poem aloud. Work together with children to create a movement and/or sound for each line of the poem. Read the poem together, inviting children to use the movements and sounds. Assign small groups of students one line each. (They can read the lines "It's Spring! Spring! Spring!" in unison.) Read the poem aloud again, this time having each group perform a line. The trick for students will be to listen carefully so they know whose line is next. Practice until students achieve a fluid reading. Make props (use the poster art for inspiration) to use in the reading for more enjoyment.

Week 3: Closeup on Words

Divide up the text of the poem and reread it using the "my turn, your turn" approach. Read the plant names (nouns) and let students read the actions (verbs). Again, read the lines "It's Spring! Spring! Spring!" in unison. Follow up by taking a closer look at the words. Introduce nouns and verbs. Let children identify both in the poem. The use the guide books (see Week 1) to find names of other flowers. What verbs (actions) can students think of to go with their new nouns?

Week 4: Make a Collaborative Book

Create a class book of the poem by writing each line on a separate sheet of paper. Divide students into pairs or small groups and let them work together to illustrate one page. Provide reference materials to help children with their drawings. Let children take turns sharing the poem with other classes.

Flower Dictionary

Flowers have a language all their own. In the old days, if you knew each flower's meaning, the gift of a bouquet might hold a secret message. Let children create a dictionary to learn the language of flowers.

◎ Give each child a copy of page 19. Tell children to color and cut out the flowers, then glue each to a sheet of paper. Have children make a cover that says "Flower Dictionary" and put their pages together to make a book.

◎ Have children use their dictionaries to name the best flower for each occasion:

✿ Valentine's Day
✿ Fourth of July
✿ A new neighbor has just moved in
✿ A friend lost a pet
✿ A friend did something nice for you

◎ Challenge children to search for the meanings of other flowers. Let them add new pages to their flower dictionaries.

Book Break

Alison's Zinnia
by Anita Lobel (Greenwillow, 1990)

In this alphabet of flowers, "Alison acquired an amaryllis for Beryl. Beryl bought a begonia for Crystal," and so on until the circular pattern brings us back to the beginning with, "Zena zeroed in on a Zinnia for Alison."

If I Could Be a Flower

Introduce children to an assortment of flowers with this pocket chart song.

◎ Collect pictures of flowers from magazines or seed catalogs. Make sure you have at least one per student. Show the pictures to children and share each flower's name. Ask: *If you could be a flower, which one would you be?*

◎ Let each child choose one flower picture. Have children paste a picture of themselves in the center of their flower. Glue the flowers to sentence strips and record each flower's name.

◎ Write the words to the following song on sentence strips and place them in the pocket chart:

> If I could be a flower,
> A flower, a flower,
> If I could be a flower, what kind would I be?
> A daisy, a pansy, a tulip, a lilac,
> If I could be a flower, I would be a _____.

Sing the song with children to the tune of "The More We Get Together." Let children take turns placing their flowers in the blank space and leading the song.

Book Break

Fran's Flower
by Lisa Bruce (HarperCollins, 1999)

When Fran finds a flowerpot with a tiny sprout inside, she becomes determined to make the flower grow. Deciding that it is hungry, she feeds it all of her favorite foods: pizza, cheeseburgers, spaghetti, chocolate chip cookies, and ice cream. After teaching children what flowers *really* need to grow, invite them to create a "balanced meal" for a plant by drawing and pasting pictures of soil, water, air, and sun on a paper plate. Conduct experiments where you deprive plants of these conditions and observe the results.

TIP

Turn the pocket chart activity into an interactive chart by gluing the sentence strips to a sheet of posterboard. Laminate the chart and the flowers. Place a piece of Velcro® in the blank space in the song and on the back of each flower. Store the flowers in a resealable bag and staple it to the back of the posterboard. At a center, children can choose flowers to fill in the blank and practice reading the song.

Teacher Share

MATH, SCIENCE

Flower Sort

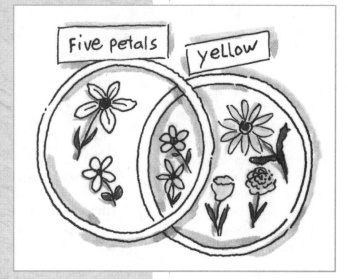

Flowers come in a wide variety of colors, shapes, and sizes. Teach children about these attributes through this sorting activity.

◎ Have each child bring a flower to school. (Have extras on hand to share.) Provide time for children to examine their flowers closely. Ask them to name attributes that tell about their flower. Record each attribute—for example, *scented, red, yellow, orange, five petals, six petals, thorns, leaves*—on a separate index card.

◎ Gather children in a seated circle. Place two hula hoops in the center so they overlap to create a Venn diagram. Place one attribute card next to each circle. Invite children to place their flowers in the Venn diagram accordingly. For example, if the two cards chosen were "red" and "scented," red flowers would go in the red circle, scented flowers would go in the scented circle and red, scented flowers would go in the space where the circles intersect. All other flowers would be placed outside of the diagram.

◎ Once the flowers are sorted, ask children what information they can gather from looking at the Venn diagram. Repeat the procedure several times using different attribute cards.

Natalie Vaughn
Phoenix School
Encinitas, California

TIP

Check with local florists who may be willing to donate slightly aged flowers for educational use.

Book Break

The Reason for a Flower
by Ruth Heller (Price Stern Sloan, 1983)

Rhyming verse and elaborate illustrations explain plant reproduction and the purpose of a flower in this charming book.

CoMPuter Connection

To view a photograph that compares the size of the Rafflesia to a boy, visit

www.senckenber g.uni-frankfurt. de/private/ gwinter/rafl.htm

MATH, SCIENCE

A Flower SO Big!

The largest flower in the world is the *Rafflesia*, which can be found in Indonesia. Help children discover just how big this flower is by going on an Internet scavenger hunt. Start at **www.didyouknow.com/flowers.htm**. Help children navigate the site to find answers to these questions:

◎ What is the name of the biggest flower in the world? (*Rafflesia Arnoldi*)

◎ How long are the petals? (*1 foot 6 inches long*)

◎ How thick are the petals? (*1 inch thick*)

◎ What does it weigh? (*15 pounds*)

◎ Where does it grow? (*Sumatra Island in Indonesia*)

Go further by investigating the smallest flower. (*Duckweed*) Ask: *How could you see a flower this tiny?* (with a microscope)

Teacher Share

SCIENCE, ART

Flower Puzzles

Teach children about the parts of a flower. Then, let them show what they have learned by creating a flower puzzle.

◎ Draw a flower on a sheet of chart paper. Work together with children to label the roots, stem, petals, sepals, pistil, and stamens.

◎ Give each child a 6- by 12-inch piece of oaktag. Ask children to draw, color, and label a flower of their own design.

◎ Demonstrate how to draw and cut out six to eight intersecting lines on the reverse side to form puzzle pieces. Have children label each piece with their name and place the puzzle pieces in a resealable bag. Invite them to exchange puzzles and use their knowledge of the parts of a flower to put them back together.

Kathy Gerber
Ravinia Elementary School
Highland Park, Illinois

My Name Is Georgia: A Portrait
by Jeanette Winter (Silver Whistle, 1998)

Written in first person, this picture-book portrait tells the story of Georgia O'Keeffe, a strong-minded girl who grew up to be a famous artist.

Teacher Share

ART

Let's Paint Flowers!

Georgia O'Keeffe painted BIG flowers so other people would notice! Use her work to inspire children to create their own mural of flowers. Begin by reading books about her life (see Book Break, above) and sharing some of her artwork.

Collect several pictures of flowers from magazines or seed catalogs. Let each child choose one flower to study and paint. Tape a long piece of mural paper to the wall. Let children take turns painting their BIG flowers on the mural. Have them sign their name under their flower just as an artist would. When they are finished, you'll have a beautiful classroom garden too big for anyone to miss!

Frank Murphy
Newton Elementary School
Newton, Pennsylvania

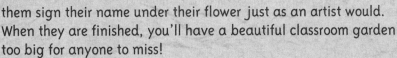

Teacher Share

Watch Us Grow!

In this movement activity, children "grow" from a seed to a flower and then become part of a bouquet. Start by asking children to scrunch down with their hands covering their faces. Explain that they're seeds that have just been planted. Pretend to cover the seeds with dirt and water them. Hold up an orange ball (or orange construction-paper sun) and let the sun shine on the seeds. The "flowers" should start to sprout by slowly standing and then bloom by removing their hands from their faces and spreading their arms open wide. As you pick the "flowers," let children form a bouquet by gathering together in a bunch.

Pam Snyder
Sissie Cares Preschool
Weston, West Virginia

"How Does Our Garden Grow?" Mini-Play

Introduce children to the concept of pollination with this easy-to-read play. The play is best done in a Readers Theater format. Place children in small groups of six. Assign each member of the group a different part and let them take turns practicing their lines. Have each group create simple props for a performance. For example, create simple flower masks by cutting the center from paper plates and gluing petals all around. Add pipe cleaner antennae to construction-paper headbands for bee and butterfly costumes. Wings for all three creatures can be cut from paper bags and taped to the child's back.

Wisteria
❀ Welcome ❀

Rose
❀ Love ❀

Nasturtium
❀ Patriotism ❀

Flower Dictionary

Snowdrop
❀ Hope ❀

Cowslip
❀ Thoughtfulness ❀

How Does Our Garden Grow?

by Jacqueline Clarke

Characters: Hummingbird ❀ Bee ❀ Butterfly ❀ Columbine ❀ Marigold ❀ Daylily

Setting: a Garden

Bee, Butterfly, Hummingbird: Let's visit the garden
For something to eat.
We'll search for flowers
With nectar so sweet.

Bee: Bright YELLOW flowers
Are my favorite kind.
I'll buzz around and around
And see what I find.

Marigold: Look no further,
I'm yellow as can be!
My name is Marigold.
Pick me! Pick me!

Hummingbird: Bright RED flowers
Are my favorite kind.
I'll dart around and around
And see what I find.

Columbine: Look no further,
I'm red as can be!
My name is Columbine.
Pick me! Pick me!

Butterfly: Bright PINK flowers
Are my favorite kind.
I'll flutter around and around
And see what I find.

Daylily: Look no further,
I'm pink as can be!
My name is Daylily.
Pick me! Pick me!

Bee, Butterfly, Hummingbird: We've each met our match.
Now it's time for a drink.
To our friends the flowers—
Dressed in yellow, red,
and pink.

Marigold, Columbine, Daylily: Sip your nectar right here,
But take the pollen to go.
Carry it to the next flower,
So new seeds will grow!

Bee, Butterfly, Hummingbird: Together we'll work
With our flower friends
To create a garden
That never ends!

Who's Afraid of the Big Bad Wolf?

Children's literature isn't always kind to animals. Coyotes, wolves, and foxes are often portrayed as villains or tricksters. In this activity, children examine the stereotype of the wolf as seen in traditional tales. They will then read nonfiction to discover what wolves are really like.

◎ Create a T-chart with the headings "Storybook Wolf" and "Real-Life Wolf." Read books with wolves as characters and list adjectives to describe them in the "Storybook Wolf" column. Read nonfiction books about wolves and list adjectives to describe them in the "Real-Life Wolf" column.

◎ Compare the two columns. How are storybook wolves different from real-life wolves? How are they the same? Is the stereotype of the "big bad wolf" accurate? Write a fictional tale with children about a wolf. Base the character on the information they have learned about real-life wolves.

Book Break

I Spy a Lion: Animals in Art

by Lucy Micklethwait (Greenwillow, 1994)

This book inspires children to look closely at great works of art as they search for animals and birds featured in the paintings.

SCIENCE, ART

I Spy Endangered Animals

Create a collage with children to bring about awareness of endangered animals.

◎ Collect pictures of endangered animals from magazines, coloring books, or the Internet.

◎ Let children work together to glue the pictures to posterboard to create a collage. They can add details and a background to complete the picture.

◎ Dispay the collage outside the classroom and title it "I Spy Endangered Animals." Write the following on a sentence strip and post it underneath the collage: *I spy a/an* _____.

◎ Each day, fill in the blank with a different endangered animal featured in the collage. (Write the animal's name on a sentence strip trimmed to fit.) Fellow students and staff members will enjoy trying to spy the animals as they learn which ones need our help.

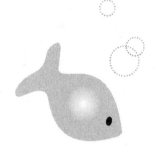

Five Little Goldfish Math Story Mat

Pet owners have a responsibility to the animals in their care. As you share this number rhyme with children, they will quickly realize what can happen when pets don't receive the care they need.

Give each child a fishbowl math story mat (see page 26) and five fish-shaped crackers. Read aloud the following rhyme while children manipulate the crackers accordingly:

Five Little Goldfish

Five little goldfish
From the pet store,
Mother forgot to feed them
And then there were four.

Four little goldfish
As hungry as can be,
Father fed them too much
And then there were three.

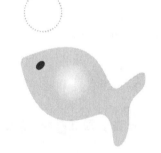

Three little goldfish
With bellies full of food,
Brother forgot to clean the bowl
And then there were two.

Two little goldfish
Not having any fun,
Sister dropped one in the sink
And then there was one.

One little goldfish
Left all alone to swim,
The family learned their lesson
And took good care of him!

TIP

Check for allergies before allowing students to snack on the crackers.

Create other addition and subtraction story problems for children to solve using the crackers and math story mat. Let children snack on their goldfish as you share five final subtraction stories. Watch them all disappear this time!

MATH

Dog Biscuit Bakery

Let children take turns measuring and adding the
ingredients in the following recipe to make dog biscuits to
donate to a local animal shelter.

Dog Biscuits

2 cups whole wheat flour   1/4 cup sunflower seeds
1/4 cup cornmeal   2 tablespoons vegetable oil
1/2 cup soy flour   1/4 cup unsulfured molasses
1 teaspoon bone meal   2 eggs mixed with 1/4 cup milk
1 teaspoon sea salt

◎ Mix dry ingredients and sunflower seeds in a large bowl.

◎ Add oil, molasses, and egg mixture (all but one
tablespoon). Add more flour if the dough is not firm enough.

◎ Knead dough for 5 minutes. Let it rest for 30 minutes.

◎ Roll out dough to a 1/2-inch thickness. Use cookie cutters
to cut the dough in shapes. Brush biscuits with remaining
egg mixture.

◎ Bake on an ungreased cookie sheet at 350° Fahrenheit for 30
minutes (or until lightly browned). For harder biscuits, turn
off the oven and leave the cookie sheet in for another hour.

◎ Store the biscuits in a tin, tie with ribbons, and deliver to
the animal shelter.

TIP

You may want to
coordinate a tour of
your local animal
shelter with the delivery
of the dog biscuits.

Book Break

Arthur's Pet Business
by Marc Brown (HarperCollins, 1990)

Before Arthur can get a pet, he must prove he is responsible. He starts a pet
business in hopes that his parents will see that he is not only responsible,
but knows how to handle animals. His business is a success, and in the end
he makes a profit *and* gains a puppy.

Teacher Share

SCIENCE

Welcome to the Pet Show!

Try this fun alternative to a live pet show!

◎ Ask each child to spend time observing and researching a pet (one of their own or someone else's). Have children draw and color a life-size cutout of the animal, write about the care and feeding habits of the pet, and record the information on the back of the picture.

◎ On the day of the pet show, act as the host and introduce each pet and his or her owner as they "lead" or carry their pet onstage.

Judy Meagher
Bozeman Schools
Bozeman, Montana

SOCIAL STUDIES

Do Animals Have Feelings?

Children might be surprised to find that animals have feelings, too. Ask them how they can tell what a cat is feeling. How about a dog? Write scenarios such as the following on slips of paper and place them in a box.

You are a cat and someone has stepped on your tail.
You are a dog and your water bowl is empty.
You are a rabbit. Someone places you in his or her lap and pets you.

Let children take turns acting out scenarios. Have other students try to guess what is happening.

Book Break

Be Gentle!
by Virginia Miller (Candlewick Press, 1999)

Bartholomew has a new kitten. But his bear hugs and games are a bit too much for his new playmate. Feeling sad that his new friend has run away, he retreats to his hiding place under the bed, where he finds the kitten!

Handle With Care

How should bugs be treated? Explore this question with children by sharing the following poem and a technique for safely removing insects from their home.

Ask children what they think the poet does when she sees a bug. Let them share how they feel about bugs outside and bugs inside. Teach them this technique for removing a bug from their home. Place a cup over the bug and slip an index card or piece of cardboard gently underneath. Carry the bug outdoors and let it go. Give each child a cup, an index card, and a plastic bug and let them practice this technique.

Hurt No Living Thing

Hurt no living thing;
Ladybird, nor butterfly,
Nor moth with dusty wing,
Nor cricket chirping cheerily,
Nor grasshopper so light of leap,
Nor dancing gnat, nor beetle fat,
Nor harmless worms that creep.

by Christina Rossetti

Teacher Share

SOCIAL STUDIES

Comparing Animals and Humans

By using a Venn diagram to compare animals and humans, children realize that their needs and wants are similar.

◎ Create a Venn diagram on a sheet of posterboard by drawing an outline of a paw print and a handprint so they intersect in the middle. Label the paw print "Animal Needs" and the handprint "Human Needs." Discuss the difference between a "need" and a "want."

◎ Ask children to name different needs. Sort them accordingly using the Venn diagram. How many needs do animals and humans share? What needs belong to animals alone? humans? Repeat this activity with animal and human "wants."

Bob Krech
Dutch Neck School
Princeton Junction, New Jersey

Name _____

Date _____

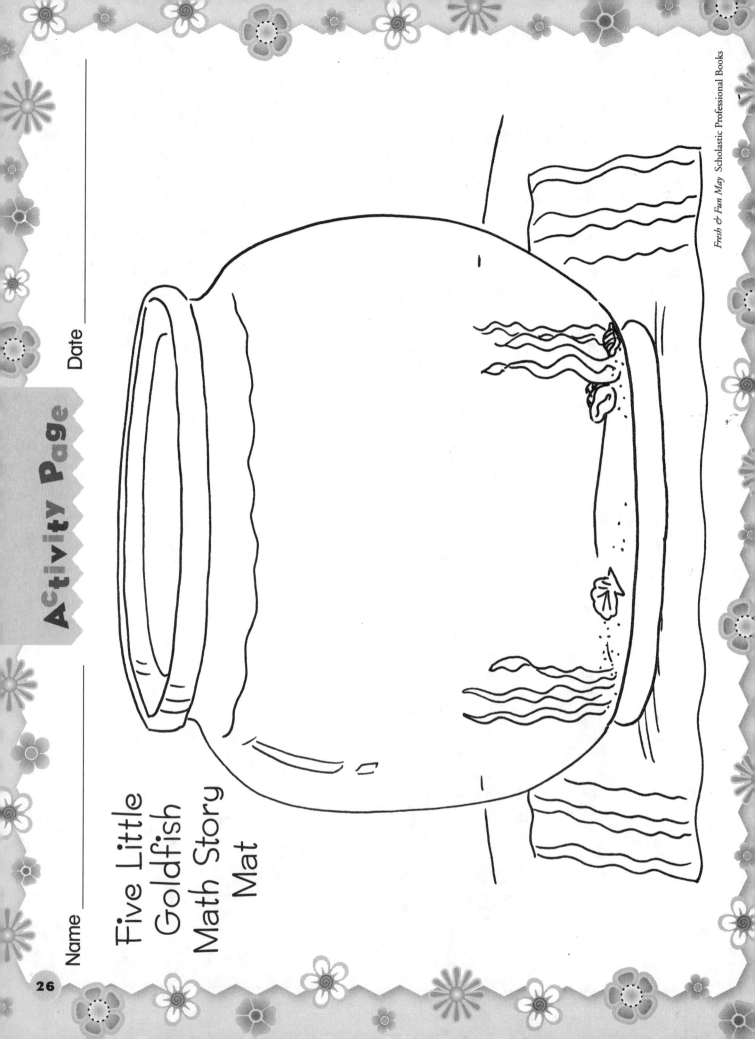

Five Little
Goldfish
Math Story
Mat

Fresh & Fun May Scholastic Professional Books

LANGUAGE ARTS

I'm in the Dictionary!

Interviewers often ask, *What one word describes you?* Pose this question to children, then have them use a dictionary to learn more about the word they choose (its meaning and part of speech). Let children share their words on a collaborative banner. Give each child a copy of page 30. Have children complete the rhyme, then color and cut out the pattern. Tape the patterns side by side so that "hands" touch. Display on a wall, then invite children to read aloud their rhymes. Ask them to share the word's meaning and part of speech with the class. Did more children choose nouns, adjectives, or verbs to describe themselves?

COMPUTER Connection

Students can use Merriam-Webster's online dictionary at **www.m-w.com** to look up their words.

Teacher Share

SCIENCE, MATH

Fingerprint Detectives

Each person's fingerprint is unique. However, fingerprints generally fall into three categories: *arch*, *whorl*, and *loop*. In this activity, children discover their dominant fingerprint type and compare it with classmates'.

Place washable-ink pads, a roll of paper towels, and copies of the record sheet (see page 31) at a center. Let each child use the ink pad to stamp a fingerprint in each box (one for each finger). Help children identify and record each fingerprint type using the illustrations at the bottom of the page. Have them determine their dominant fingerprint type (the one that occurs most often) from the data they collected. Create a graph to determine which fingerprint type is the most and which is the least common in the class.

Andrea Page
Terry A. Taylor School
Spencerport, New York

TIP

Children can also make fingerprints with this fun method: Press your finger on a smooth surface, such as a file cabinet, and sprinkle with powder. Gently blow the powder away to reveal a fingerprint!

Book Break

Chrysanthemum

by Kevin Henkes (Greenwillow, 1991)

Chrysanthemum believed she had the perfect name. Then she started school and her friends made flower jokes and pointed out that her name was as long as half the alphabet. But with the help of Miss Delphinium, the music teacher, Chrysanthemum blooms once again. Follow up with "Names Add Up," below.

Let children find out the meaning and origin of their name as well as the most popular first names in America at

4babynames. 4anything.com

Teacher Share

MATH

Names Add Up

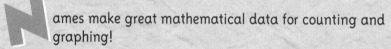

Names make great mathematical data for counting and graphing!

◎ Give each child a copy of the record sheet. (See page 32.) Ask children to record their first, middle, and last name in the spaces provided. Have them calculate the total for each name.

◎ Challenge children to write a number sentence based on the number of letters in their first and last name. Can they find another student with the same sum but a different combination?

◎ Use the data collected on their first names only to create class graphs. Which name has the most letters? Do more children have an odd or even number of letters?

Colleen Huston
Confidence Elementary School
Redhouse, Virginia

SOCIAL STUDIES, ART

Calendar Sticks

Native Americans of the Southwest recorded history using calendar sticks: pictures drawn or carved on flat sticks. Invite children to create their own calendar sticks. Give each child a flat stick or strip of posterboard. For each of seven days, let children draw one picture to mark an important event. At the end of the week, let children share events on their calendar sticks.

Another Important Book
by Margaret Wise Brown (HarperCollins, 1999)

This sequel to *The Important Book* examines the "important" things about ages one to six. For example, "The important thing about being one is that life has just begun," and "The important thing about two is all the things that you can do." Have children think back to their "younger" days and recall one important event for each age. Let them record these events in pictures and words on a time line. Set aside time for each child to share with the class.

Teacher Share

SOCIAL STUDIES

My Life in a Suitcase

We carry our personal histories with us wherever we go. In this activity, children will literally pack theirs into a suitcase to share with others. Begin by sharing your own personal history with children. Gather several items from home that symbolize different aspects of your life—for example:

◎ photographs

◎ diplomas and teaching credentials

◎ favorite books

◎ objects that represent hobbies/interests

◎ a recipe for a favorite family food

◎ maps showing where your family came from

Place the items in a suitcase and bring it in to school. Invite children to listen as you unpack your suitcase and reveal each object's significance. Throughout the next few weeks, set aside time for each student to fill and share his or her own "suitcase." To simplify the procedure, you may have students select items that will fit in a paper lunch bag. Explain that although we each have things in common with others, our personal histories are unique.

Marianne Chang
A. L. Schilling School
Newark, California

I'm in the Dictionary!
Collaborative Banner

I'm in the dictionary,
Look and see!

is the word
that tells about me!

Fresh & Fun May Scholastic Professional Books

Name _____ Date _____

Fingerprint Detectives

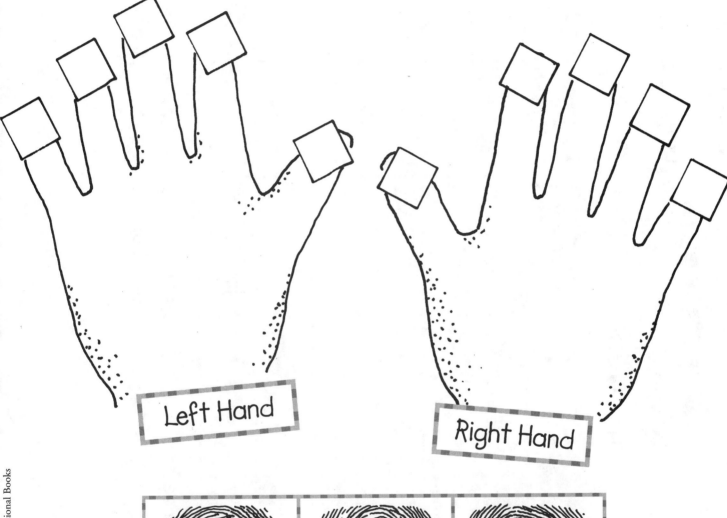

Left Hand

Right Hand

arch   loop   whorl

My fingerprint type is _____.

Names Add Up

	Number of Letters	Odd or Even?	Number of Consonants	Number of Vowels
First Name				
Middle Name				
Last Name				

◎ Write a number sentence to represent the number of letters in your first and last name:

◎ Find another student with the same sum but a different combination.

Name _____

Fresh & Fun May Scholastic Professional Books